On the Shore of West Hill Pond

Joseph Conaci

2014

Camp Workcoeman
New Hartford, Connecticut

Copyright 2013–2014 Joseph Conaci.
All photographs are in the public domain.

Edited by Matthew Petroff.
Typeset in 12 pt EB Garamond using LaTeX.

Preface

As part of the celebration of Camp Workcoeman's ninetieth anniversary, I wrote the vignettes contained herein. Each story can stand alone, but the reader will gain a better understanding of the early development of camp by examining every one in the published order. Citations were eliminated from this booklet to reduce publication costs; however, references are available upon request. I owe a debt to many people who provided historical documents and photographs for this publication, but I especially wish to thank Matthew Petroff for assisting in microfilm research and typesetting the booklet.

Joseph Conaci
29 June 2014

Contents

Beginnings of Scouting 1

Early Torrington Troops 3

Establishing a Council 5

Camp Pioneer and Hikes 7

Frank Elmer Coe 11

History of the Land 15

Preparing the Camp 19

The First Season 21

The Second Season 25

Scout Mothers' Auxiliary 27

A Renewed Council 31

1928 Season 33

Forming a Countywide Council 37

Northern Litchfield County Council	39
1930 Season	41
Effect of the Great Depression	45
Visitors and Baseball	49
Three Cheers for Old Workcoeman	51
Dining Hall Expansion Plans	55
The Silver Jubilee	57
Council Executives	61
Palmer Liddle	65
A New Dining Hall	67
1938 Season	71
Building Boom	75
Growing Nationalism	79
Economic Recovery	81
War	85
New Leadership	89
Helping the War Effort	91
Expansion	93
Post-War Prosperity	97

Beginnings of Scouting

The story of Camp Workcoeman begins with Scouting itself. Before William Boyce incorporated the Boy Scouts of America in February of 1910, various character building groups for young men already existed in the United States. Ernest Seton and Daniel Beard ran the two largest associations, the Woodcraft Indians and the Sons of Daniel Boon, respectively. When Boyce brought Robert Baden-Powell's British Scouting model to the United States, he only owned the Boy Scouts of America name and had permission to use Baden Powell's Handbook, *Scouting for Boys*. Edgar Robinson of the Young Men's Christian Association ended up providing the organizational skills and the national network to get the BSA off the ground. Robinson pulled Seton, Beard, and two other Scouting associations together to form a nationwide movement.

While Robinson was providing the first organization, the very first troops were already meeting. These groups formed along the same chaotic lines as the National Council. Often boys from a civic club or church started a patrol; some used *Scouting for Boys* before 1910. Sometimes these troops did not receive official charters from the national office in New York City, and many others gathered together and split apart without the Boy Scouts of America being the wiser.

The first formally chartered troop in Litchfield County, possibly in Connecticut, was made up of the boys of the First Baptist Church,

WINSTED SCOUTS ON A HIKE AROUND 1910: Of the eleven Scouts in the photo, twelve if the photographer is included, some may be, Stanly Colt, Lester McFarland, Harold Sanford, Willys Sanford, Harold Smith, or Ralph Smith.

in Winsted. The Reverend Franklin Elmer provided the momentum for the troop and served as Scoutmaster.

Early Torrington Troops

Edgar Robinson handed over the reins of the Boy Scouts of America to James West in 1911, but the nationwide connections with the Young Men's Christian Association persisted. In Torrington, a troop was formed out of the local YMCA in the spring on 1911, with four patrols by the end of April. Most of the Scouts were congregants from the Methodist Church. For its first trip on 12 May 1911, the troop hiked some of the distance from Torrington to West Hill Pond, staying overnight near where Camp Workcoeman is today.

The troop was very active in 1911, marching in Torrington's Memorial Day Parade, camping at the Goshen Fair, and searching for a lost three-year-old. However, records drop off during 1912, and the troop disbanded sometime late that year, or in 1913. The YMCA troop reformed in March of 1914 and received a charter as Troop 1, Torrington in April.

Troop 1 slowly grew to a size of around forty scouts, but in 1916 and 1917 interest in Scouting picked up. The National Council chartered four more troops in Torrington, out of Trinity Episcopal Church, Center Congregational Church, and the Methodist Episcopal Church. During the first decade of Scouting in the United States, summer camps of a week or more were usually the responsibility of the troop's Scoutmaster. While earlier long-term camps may have occurred, the first record of one for the Scouts of Torrington was during

TORRINGTON YMCA: The Main Street building where the Torrington YMCA was quartered from 1890 until the present structure was built in 1922; photograph by the Karl Brothers Studio of Litchfield.

the summer of 1916. Scoutmaster L. H. Avery and his wife organized the camp on the shore of the Otis Reservoir in Massachusetts.

Establishing a Council

The first five troops in Torrington interacted directly with the national office, through its Field Department in New York. However, there were troubles with this arrangement. The Scouters in the established troops only received answers to program and policy questions by writing to the national office. To maintain this arrangement, the national office would need to hire an army of bureaucrats. Additionally, the New York office could not possibly know about all the potential troop sponsors, much less devise a way to recruit them. To come up with a solution, the national office used the same sort of franchise type system that worked with troops. Each community organization, which chartered a troop, chose a representative. These representatives then joined together with other interested men to become members of a local council.

The national office offered two options, a First Class Council managed by a paid professional Scouter, or a Second Class Council managed by a volunteer Commissioner. Implicit in this agreement was that if a community opted for a Second Class Council, it would ultimately advance in rank and hire a professional. Regardless, the troops could receive unit service locally, whether or not the council program was organized under a Council Executive or a Commissioner, all without adding to the piles of unanswered mail in the Field Department.

TROOP 4: Members of Troop 4 pose in front of the Methodist Episcopal Church in Torrington, during the 1920s. Note the variation in uniforms between the Scouters and the boys, as styles of uniforms transitioned during the early 1920s.

In March of 1917, Torrington Scouters and other supporters met with Carl Northrup, the Waterbury Council Executive. The men present showed the varying interests in the Borough of Torrington, not just the delegates from the YMCA, the Episcopal Church, the Congregational Church, and the Methodist Church, but also lawyers, merchants, tradesmen, and manufacturers. With Northrup's help, they elected to form a Second Class Council and set out to recruit a Commissioner.

Camp Pioneer and Hikes

The Torrington Council reorganized in March of 1920 as a First Class Council. Even before the council officers completed the charter application, they hired Torrington's Assistant Postmaster, William Copley, as a part-time executive. Among Copley's first tasks was to arrange a summer program. Around the same time, the Hartford Council purchased fifty acres on West Hill Pond for Camp Pioneer. Copley struck a deal with Hartford Council Executive Sherman Ripley for Torrington Scouts to join in on the Camp Pioneer program. The Torrington Council paid for the Scouts' first week; local service organizations such as the Torrington Rotary Club volunteered in the camp's development.

The troop response was overwhelming, to the point that during the first week of camp the carpenters the Hartford Council hired to build the camp office had to construct more tables for the dining hall instead. Later in the summer, the camp was so overbooked that some Scouts bunked in the dining hall. More than seventy of the Torrington Council's one hundred and ten Scouts attended, and many stayed for multiple weeks.

The downside of this popularity was that for the 1921 season the Hartford Council reserved Camp Pioneer for Hartford County Scouts. Improvising, William Copley planed a pair of hikes. The first trek was about sixty miles—one week to walk from Torrington

TORRINGTON SCOUTS ON A COUNCIL HIKE IN 1921 OR 1922

to the Old New-Gate Prison and back. The second, longer hike was a two-week circuit of the northwest hills. On this longer trek, some of the boys suffered a reaction to poison ivy. According to Seymour Weeks, because of this: "Mr. Copley...decided to lay over a while at Bantam Lake, since we were ahead of schedule. He found a good spot and we camped near Mr. Frank Coe's cottage. Mr. Coe watched us and he was, if I might say so, rather impressed by the way we conducted ourselves."

Taking a break from hiking

Frank Elmer Coe

Frank Elmer Coe was born to Nelson and Caroline (née Workman) Coe on 1 February 1872. Raised in Torrington, Frank Coe attended public schools in town, and received some higher education in Nebraska. After two semesters at Doane College, Frank Coe returned to Torrington to manage his father's business. The Coe Furniture Company, founded by Frank Coe's grandfather, specialized in home goods. Under Frank Coe's administration, the corporation branched out into retail, including bicycle sales and repair. Frank Coe married Jennie A. Ford on 3 April 1895; they had one son together, Franklin Earl Coe, in May of 1897.

In 1899, Frank Coe sold the furniture company, and the following year he got a job at the Warrenton Woolen Mill. The mill was managed by two of Coe's uncles and specialized in manufacturing kersey cloth, mostly for police, postal, and navy uniforms.

Starting as a wool grader, Coe worked his way up through the organization. By the time the new Main Street factory opened in 1908, he was an officer of the corporation. When the company recapitalized in 1911 and over the next decade, he purchased additional shares, eventually gaining control of the mill as he rose from secretary, to treasurer and, ultimately, to president.

Frank Coe took an interest in community affairs; he was a member of the Rotary Club, the town board of relief, President of the

Torrington Wheel Club, and Exalted Ruler of the Elks. Until 1923 Torrington had two governments, a town government that serviced the rural areas, and a borough government that maintained services in the built up areas around the factories. Coe served the borough as a burgess (selectman) during the 1910s; in 1917 he was elected Warden, a position similar to that of mayor. Coe served on both the Democratic Town Committee and the party's state committee; he was considered for the 1920 Gubernatorial nomination, but declined. In 1923, he lost in Torrington's first citywide mayoral election.

In the early 1920s, Frank Coe joined the executive board of the new Torrington Boy Scout Council, and in April of 1923, the members elected Coe Council President. As president, Coe worked to establish a council camping program, but he put his efforts on hold when the Council Executive resigned. Frank Coe searched throughout New England for a trained, experienced professional and recruited Earl C. Beebe from the Greater Providence Council. With a camp man on board, Coe searched for a location in the hills around Torrington. On 24 May 1924, Coe purchased land fronting West Hill Pond in New Hartford. He named the property after his recently deceased mother; by inserting his father's name between the two syllables of his mother's name, he created the unique word *Workcoeman*.

A mere four days later, Frank Coe died of heart failure. At the memorial service, Council Executive Beebe served as one of the pallbearers. Members of the civic clubs Coe was active in attended, along with mill employees and the city's police and fire departments. At the burial, a Boy Scout honor guard escorted the body to the grave.

Frank E. Coe

History of the Land

The new Workcoeman property was situated just south of the New Hartford-Barkhamsted town line, at the end of an old logging road. During the nineteenth century, the land was primarily used as a wood lot, supplying timber for the barns and fences of local farms. Around the turn of the twentieth century, the trees were cut for charcoal, to feed the forges of Connecticut's metallurgical industries. After loggers felled the trees, they dragged them to a charcoal hearth where the wood was covered with layers of leaves and earth. Colliers lit the buried wood and tended the fire, letting in just enough air to boil off the water and burn off the tar and volatile oils. In about two weeks, the colliers produced a nearly pure carbon fuel. The long burning fires sterilized the earth, which prevented new plant growth. These charcoal hearths were some of the few open places at Workcoeman in 1924. One collier's hearth, not too far from the edge of the water, was the site of early council fires, and several incarnations later is the present amphitheater.

After a few decades of recovery, the land was densely forested with thin white birches and American beeches. Countless shoots grew out of the old red oak stumps; some survived and grew into trees with as many as seven trunks. Many of these long-lived trees are still growing; some of the most distinctive provide the canopy over the camp road. The hardy rootstock of the American chestnut also allowed for quick regrowth; however, the chestnut blight reached Northwest Connecticut in the 1910s, leaving many small, dead, standing trees by 1924. In the moister sections of camp, yellow poplars were the dominate succession species, with a few growing as large as the hemlocks. Eastern hemlocks produce terrible charcoal and, therefore, were rarely cut; left alone by the loggers, the trees towered over the hardwood saplings in the early years of camp.

The lake itself attracted settlers who built mills along the outlet early in the nineteenth century. The Greenwoods Scythe Company purchased the water rights to the pond, and their successor companies built a permanent stone dam at the outlet of the lake in 1876. This dam provided water power to the mills in New Hartford Center during the dry summer months. The high water quality of the spring fed pond also brought the attention of the New Britain Water Department, which considered West Hill Pond as a potential reservoir in the 1910s. However, recreation beat out the other potential uses. As early as 1880, the pond attracted picnickers and vacationers, and in the early 1920s, Frederick Baldwin subdivided much of the lakefront property for summer cottages. Seeing the opportunity for a Scout camp, Frank Coe purchased the five northern most lots just before his death in 1924.

Camp Workcoeman shoreline: Taken in 1924 by the Dautrich Studio.

Preparing the Camp

With Frank Coe's death, ownership of the property transferred to his wife, Jennie, and responsibility for the Scout program to Council Executive Earle Beebe. Beebe served as the first director, or Camp Chief, and he recruited Scouter Seymour Weeks as his assistant. Scouts Ralph Fox, Kenneth Green, Harold Patterson, and Thomas Wall made up the rest of the staff.

Chief Beebe camped at Workcoeman during the last two weekends in June, in order to encourage Scouts and Scouters to visit the property. In addition to the registered members, volunteers from Torrington also came up to help establish the camp. The old logging road was too narrow and uneven to drive on, and, as such, the equipment and most of the building materials were carried into camp by hand. In addition to clearing sites for the tents and digging a four-seat latrine, the volunteers built the first kitchen. This open-sided wood structure provided cover for an icebox and a World War I surplus wood-fired stove.

The five-man staff joined Chief Beebe in July, and they spent the next two weeks completing the camp. Frederick Baldwin offered the council a shack near the brook that flows in front of the present camp sign. The staff tore this structure down and used the lumber to build a storage shed. Near the kitchen and under the shade of taller trees, they set up a dining fly. In addition to a staff tent and a headquarters

ENTRANCE TO CAMP IN 1924

tent, the staff set up four camper tents. Each tent had six cots set up on a thick layer of straw, to protect the ground. The last major task before the Scouts arrived on the fourteenth of July was to set up the waterfront. The staff built a dock that stretched beyond the boulders along the shoreline and into the clear waters of the lake. Of course, the staff weeks consisted of more than just construction and setup. Chief Beebe, an officer of the Red Cross Volunteer Life Saving Corps, taught the staff lifeguarding techniques.

The First Season

Early on a warm July morning, about twenty Torrington Council Scouts made their way to Camp Workcoeman. While some may have been dropped off on West Hill Road, most of the boys took the Torrington-Winsted Trolley line. After getting dropped off near what is now Pinewoods Road, the boys walked north to West Hill Road, a mile along that, and finally another mile up the old logging road into camp. The boys may have traveled with fellow Scouts, but they did not function in their usual troops. Instead, when the Scouts arrived at camp, they settled into one of the four camper tents, and those tent mates formed the patrol they worked in for the remainder of their stay.

The hike up to camp was not the end of the walking at Camp Workcoeman. While each tent had its own washbasin, the camp itself had no potable water source. The Scouts hiked a little over a quarter of a mile to a spring and hauled cans of water back to camp. The primitive nature of the camp and the necessary details of the first season kept the Scouts busy. In addition to the customary scoutcraft activities, the boys spent much of their time building trails through the property and clearing the area around the waterfront. These sorts of programs and the name Workcoeman may have given an impression of drudgery; however, an exchange in *The Torrington Register* offers a boy's perspective of these pioneer type activities:

"Gee, it's great!"

"What's great?"

"Why, Camp Workcoeman!"

"But I thought that it was all work."

"Work? Nothing but to get up an appetite."

"Eats? Oh yes, Piles on piles of them."

The highlight of the program for most boys was West Hill Pond. With Chief Beebe's experience and the staff's training, camp program revolved around daily aquatics. Many of the Scouts who arrived on 14 July were prepared for a two-week stay, but more Scouts arrived every few days. To accommodate, the boys set up three more tents. Indeed, word of Camp Workcoeman brought new Scouts into Torrington's troops.

At the end of July, Workcoeman adjourned for two weeks. Now that Chief Beebe and the members of the Torrington Council had a little experience, they began to think long term. During the intersession, Beebe, along with Seymour Weeks and Ralph Fox, visited nine Scout camps, and fresh with ideas, they returned to open Workcoeman for two weeklong sessions. The first season ended with a flag ceremony on the evening of 31 August 1924.

CHIEF BEEBE'S TENT IN 1924: Note the wash basin to the right-hand side.

The Second Season

A mere two months after Camp Workcoeman closed for the 1924 season, Council Executive Earl Beebe resigned. It was several months before Chief Beebe found a new job as the Waterbury Council Executive, so other employment opportunities probably were not his main motivation. However, the death of Frank Coe, the Torrington Council's main benefactor, may have played a part in his decision. The executive board hired Herbert McLeod, an Assistant Scoutmaster in Troop 2, to serve as the new Council Executive and Camp Chief.

For the summer of 1925, Chief McLeod organized a program very similar to that of the 1924 season, with emphasis on aquatics and pioneering. He recruited Thomas Wall from the previous season's staff and Robert Freeman, a wilderness guide from Maine. Freeman served as chef for part of the season, but also taught canoeing. He shared his backwoods experience with the boys, and using lumber supplied by Frederick Baldwin, Freeman and the Scouts built a log cabin.

Another program that returned from 1924 was a Scout Honor Society, the Tunxis Indians. The previous season's members elected the 1925 honor campers. The members met after taps on Saturday night, and their activities were a mix of traditions from Camp Sepunkum and local lore. The honor campers were recognized with a blue tomahawk inserted into the CW of the maroon camp em-

LOG CABIN BUILT BY CAMPERS AND STAFF IN 1925: The cabin was slightly to the west of the present waterfront area.

blem. Athletic events were the other high point of 1925. Several times during the five-week season, the Scouts hiked over to the Hartford Council's Camp Pioneer. Among other inter-camp challenges, the Scouts played baseball on the diamond that the Torrington Rotary Club built in 1920. At the last game of the season, the Torrington Scouts lost to the Hartford Scouts, 6–7.

Scout Mothers' Auxiliary

The 1925 camp season may have been just as successful as the first in 1924, but behind the scenes the Torrington Council was struggling. The council only had enough funds to pay Scout Executive Herbert McLeod part-time. Often the scout office was only open evenings, because McLeod had to work elsewhere during the day. Without the support of a full-time executive, the Council's youth membership stagnated, and nearly a fifth of the Scouters dropped their registrations. This lack of engagement showed in the 1926 camp season; while Camp Workcoeman accommodated 20 boys per week in 1925, in 1926 the camp size was limited to 16 boys a week, for the same four-week season.

In 1927, Camp Workcoeman was only open for two weeklong sessions in July, and a few weekend sessions during the month of August. Because Chief McLeod was committed to his other job, Alex Goodskey, a teacher and outdoorsman, served as Camp Director. However, council volunteers used the camp season to grow Scouting in Torrington. From around the city, boys not involved in Scouting were recruited to attend camp, and also sign up as Scouts. The camping committee offered numerous facility improvements to attract more campers; in addition to tent platforms and new cots, the council completed a dining hall and kitchen that had been started the previous year. Neils Rosenbeck, Chairman of Troop 10, and John

Calder, Council Vice President, organized most of the fundraising for the new hall, but their drive also helped to secure the financial future of the council.

Frank Coe's widow, Jennie, coordinated recruiting among the registered boys, through the Scout Mothers' Auxiliary. The Auxiliary was originally an informal group, made up of Troop 2 moms, who arranged transportation for camping trips. Jennie Coe got involved late in 1926, and the organization was formalized with her as president early the next year. She tried to get every Scout mother in Torrington to join, and then encourage them to send their boys to camp. The Auxiliary was a mix of social club and fundraising arm, spending just as much time fundraising as out picnicking or at card parties. They provided camp scholarships and many of the niceties that did not fit into the council budget, ranging from curtains for the kitchen to the camp's first archery set.

Jennie Coe and several visitors, along with the camp staff, at Workcoeman in the late 1920s

A Renewed Council

In 1927, a newfound volunteer commitment financially stabilized the Torrington Council. With cash on hand, the Executive Board could hire a full-time Council Executive; however, because Herbert McLeod found his other part-time work more stable, he resigned to make way for Edward Jacot. Jacot, a veteran of the First World War, served as Scoutmaster of Troop 1 for seven years, and for the recent camp season was the assistant director and aquatics instructor.

Chief Jacot set to work immediately, starting with a promotional drive centered on a public scoutcraft exhibit at the council offices. Scouts showed off the various projects they made as part of merit badge work. At the end of the weeklong exhibit, the projects were moved to shop windows around Torrington to keep Scouting in the public eye. The highlight of the drive was a series of acts at the high school's adult education Thanksgiving show. One patrol from Troop 4 showed how to construct a signal tower, a Scout from Troop 2 demonstrated fire by friction, and other boys offered a series of Scout songs. The event sought to introduce Torrington's immigrant population, who were the primary students at the night classes, to the Scouting movement. After the publicity campaign, the council launched a membership drive; each Scout who recruited two new boys or persuaded three who had dropped registration to return received a copy of the new 1927 Scout Handbook. Chief Jacot also

SCOUTS SWIMMING AT WORKCOEMAN SOMETIME DURING THE LATE 1920S

launched the national council's new five-year training program with a course on scoutmastership.

As a vote of confidence in the reorganized council, Jennie Coe formally presented the deed to Camp Workcoeman to the council; because the council was not incorporated, Scouters Frederick Baldwin, Alfred Burg, John Calder, Frank Damon, and George Vogel formed a committee of trustees to hold the property. By the time the 1928 camp season rolled around, there were enough reservations to open Workcoeman for six weeks, and there was a good chance of beating the attendance record set in 1924, 76 Scout-weeks.

1928 Season

The 1928 camp season opened on Sunday 1 July with a great deal of promise. Reservations were far ahead of any previous year, and the Scouts had many developments to look forward to, including a radio and phonograph. Fredrick Baldwin and his Camping Committee pulled stumps from the old tenting area to create a parade ground. Chief Jacot secured a donation of a new flagpole from the American Legion, where he was an active member. As part of the first week's activities, the campers and staff raised the flagpole on the east side of the new parade ground.

    A week of camp offered boys a tightly filled schedule; camp started each morning at seven, with reveille and a voluntary swim. Then, morning colors at seven-twenty, followed by a seven-thirty breakfast. The morning's program was filled with two hours of scoutcraft, before a swimming period at eleven. Right before lunch, a staff man inspected the campers' tents for cleanliness and organization, rating each tent. After lunch, Scouts had various camp responsibilities, such as hauling water from a spring a quarter mile away. The boys carried the water to the dining hall and used it to top off the large drinking water tank. The open space that the parade ground provided meant that the Scouts could play baseball at camp, along with other games, at two o'clock. Then, as now, free swim was at four in the afternoon. Each night after dinner, the Scouts took the fleet of five boats out onto the lake, and then joined together for a campfire at eight-thirty.

Scouts occasionally broke from the schedule, weekly for an outpost trek, which usually involved a stop to play a baseball game at Camp Pioneer or Camp Sequassen. A few Scouts also hiked to the Legionaries encampment, at the new American Legion State Forest in Barkhamsted. Throughout the season, the boys constructed a swimming raft, crafted around sealed metal barrels. The Scout Mothers' Auxiliary provided a donation to get the raft started the previous fall, and when the group joined their sons for a picnic at camp, they presented $16.31 to pay for the last parts of the raft. The campers and staff finally carried the ten-foot by twelve-foot raft into the lake during the fifth week of camp. Over the summer, about a quarter of the boys in camp signed up for an addition week, making the 1928 season the most successful to that point. Seventy Scouts attended for one hundred and twenty-four boy-weeks, 163% of the 1924 record.

SCOUTS PACKING THEIR BACKPACKS ON THE PARADE GROUND, UNDER THE FLAGPOLE: This photograph was probably taken around 1930, and shows the first dining hall, now the kitchen, in the background.

Forming a Countywide Council

Torrington's renewed interest in Scouting in the late 1920s, along with a full-time Council Executive, attracted some attention from the national office in New York. The ten-year initiative to bring all troops in the nation under a local council was nearing its end. In the first six years of that plan, the number of First Class Councils more than doubled. That was the same program that brought the National Council's field staff to Torrington in 1920, to organize a First Class Council. George Fisher, deputy Chief Scout Executive, inspected Workcoeman during the summer on 1928. While he made some positive comments, he revealed his true intentions at both a Rotary Luncheon and at a council meeting, where he promoted the idea of establishing Torrington as center of a countywide council.

A larger territory meant that the Torrington Council would take responsibility for the troops dispersed throughout Litchfield County. In addition, the council and its executive would also be in charge of forming new units in communities without Scouting. This could entail increased travel expenses and possibly hiring an Assistant Council Executive. While Winsted might provide additional financial support, the fifteen other towns would probably not.

Given the likelihood of increased expenses and the lack of prospective revenue, most Torrington volunteers were wary of the proposal. On the other hand, Scouters from Kent and Warren

THE DINING HALL, NOW THE KITCHEN, IN THE LATE 1920S

showed unbridled enthusiasm, especially with the prospect of support from a local, trained, member of the professional staff. As in Torrington, the proposal did not receive a great deal support in a dozen other communities. Regardless of what the National Council thought, many volunteers in the farm villages and small mill towns felt they were doing just fine without a local council. The Scouters delayed until December, when the National Council issued an ultimatum. If the council did not expand to include all Scouts in Northwest Connecticut, the National Office would not renew the Torrington Council's Charter, and National would dissolve the organization.

Northern Litchfield County Council

In the fall of 1928, the National Office pressured the Torrington Council to expand and include sixteen additional towns in northwest Connecticut. The volunteers in Torrington were wary of the additional expense, and troops in the outlying towns were not particularly keen on a local council. Impatient with the tactics of delay, the National Office threatened to incorporate the entire area into the Waterbury Council.

The members of the Torrington Council conceded, and troops from Kent and Warren were made formal members of the council on the last Friday in December of 1928. To reflect this expanded mission, the council voted to change its name to the Northern Litchfield County Council, and to incorporate. John Calder, as chairman of the Troop Organization Committee, along with Commissioner F. Earle Coe and Council Executive Edward Jacot, traveled throughout Litchfield County to persuade Scouters to affiliate with the council. They offered the service of a Scout professional and the summer program at Workcoeman. In the farm communities, where Scouts often had to work during the summer, camp was not much of an incentive. Even with the council advantages, the individual troops would loose some of their independence, and their identity—come rechartering time,

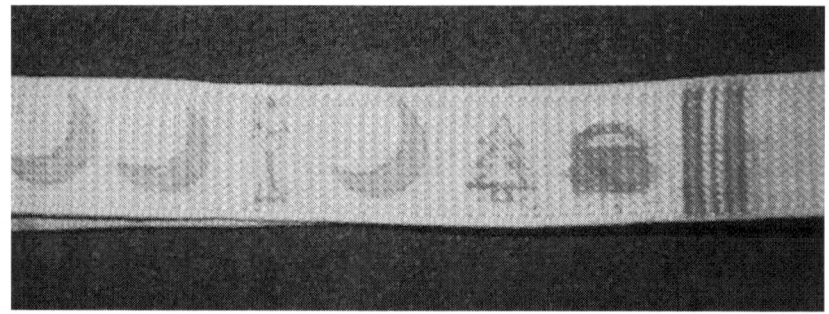

A SCOUT BELT: The various stamped emblems each represent some form of camp achievement. Although probably not from Workcoeman, this type of belt recognition was introduced at camp in 1929.

the various Troop 1s in each town would be assigned new numbers. After four months of promotion, only the West Cornwall Troop joined the council. Eventually Camp Workcoeman won over the Winsted Scouters, but by then the National Council had enough of the dithering. In July of 1929 they transferred eleven more towns to the Northern Litchfield County Council.

On the seventh of July Camp Workcoeman opened, with Scouts from Kent, Torrington, and Warren in attendance. With more boys from Torrington than the previous year, and Scouts from additional towns, the dining hall that had been adequate just two years prior was crowded. The number of seats in the dining hall set the capacity of Workcoeman at forty-four. With space at a premium, the staff set up a twenty-foot by thirty-foot tent and a thirty-foot square tent to accommodate rainy day activities. The highlight for Scouts in the second week was when they had the opportunity to take over the camp. For one day, various Scouts served as Camp Chief, counselors for swimming, boating, and handicraft, and even chef.

1930 Season

The fifteen towns added to the Northern Litchfield County Council in 1929 more than doubled the potential Boy Scouts who might attend Camp Workcoeman. Of course, the council would have to form troops and enroll Scouts before any increase in camp attendance. As in 1927, the camp program was a large part of the recruiting effort. The council heavily promoted the 1930 season, focusing on the new aspects of the camp program. Most of these new programs started off with donations from local businesses. With a leather craft kit and metalworking tools, Workcoeman offered a greatly expanded handicraft program. Two bows, twelve arrows, and one target amounted to a complete archery inventory. However, most of the camp program remained unchanged, consisting of a mix of aquatics, sports, and scoutcraft. A new variation in the aquatics program was water polo, which the Scouts played during four o'clock free swim. The number of Scouts in camp, more than forty, was a bit large to continue the tradition of a weekly overnight trek, but the entire camp still day-hiked out to a local farm for lunch each Thursday. Scouts from Canaan, Cornwall, Litchfield, Torrington, Warren, and even New York helped to make 1930 another record-breaking season. However, attendance was not quite as high as planned, and a large and unexpected outlay contributed to a five hundred dollar deficit for the season.

In the fall of 1929, the spring used as a drinking water supply for the past six seasons failed a test. In order to get a new water supply, the council would have to drill a well, but the logging road leading to camp was much too rough to bring in the drilling equipment. By the time enough fill was hauled to West Hill and the new road graded, winter set in. Fredrick Baldwin paid the four hundred dollars to build the road, since it would help sell his remaining lots along the west shore of the lake. In January, the council conducted its annual fund drive with an addition $1,000 to pay for the well; however, the drive came up short. The council continued quietly soliciting donations through the spring, but finally contracted to drill the well in June, with Fredrick Baldwin covering the shortfall. As part of this informal arrangement, people along the lake could get water at the camp well for their summer cottages. An additional fund drive in the fall balanced the Northern Litchfield County Council's books, but the difficulty of that year made the recession very obvious, which would limit the growth of the camp for the next several years.

CAMP EMBLEM USED DURING THE 1930S: These earned patches were called letters, and held the dual requirement of proficiency in camping and completing work that added, "permanent value to the camp." In practice, very few of these emblems were awarded, and mostly to members of the camp staff. Other Scouts received recognitions to be worn on their belt, a bar for each year as a camper, and a star for each addition week attended.

Effect of the Great Depression

The prosperity of the 1920s facilitated new programs and modern equipment at Camp Workcoeman. The breadth of the economic crisis of 1929 was not immediately apparent to the Scouters of the Northern Litchfield County Council. However, in 1930 the campaign to raise money to grade the camp road and drill a well fell flat. In addition to the problems funding camp projects, the annual council fund drive came up short, by nearly a quarter of the goal. The 1931 fund drive was more ambitious, seeking to make up for the previous year's loss with a higher goal. While the 1931 drive raised an additional four hundred and sixty-nine dollars, percentage-wise the fundraiser was even less successful. These difficulties were endemic of the 1930s; the troubles of raising money exposed deflation. In deflation, the amount of money available for transactions drops, and because of the slow rate at which the economy can adjust to the smaller money supply, deflation strangles the economy. For the Scouts in Connecticut, this meant it was very difficult to get together the funds for a week of camp. As long as deflation rode on the economy, the Council would find it difficult to fund its programs and expand Camp Workcoeman.

In 1930, the large-scale unemployment that characterized the Great Depression was not yet widespread, hovering around 5.4%. But in 1931, as the depression worsened and businesses closed, the unemployed rate rose. Torrington's corporate leaders, who were some of the most active Scouters, spent much more of their time trying to keep their businesses afloat. For example, in March, F. Earle Coe resigned as Council Commissioner to devote his time to keeping the Warrenton Woolen Mill out of bankruptcy. In spite of these monetary problems, the Northern Litchfield County Council continued to grow and in May of 1931 reached a record number of five hundred Scouts and one hundred and seventy Scouters. This new registration height was mostly thanks to three new units, Troop 22 in Canaan, Troop 23 in West Torrington, and Troop 24 in Sharon.

The larger council enrollment helped to maintain Camp Workcoeman's 1931 attendance at 1920s levels. For the Scouts in camp, the program showed no signs of the ongoing business depression. Archery, introduced the previous year, was quite popular, and thanks to a donation from Jennie Coe, the archery inventory doubled. Other citizens still wanted to support the camp program, but because of the deflation, many of the gifts were in kind. For example, Arthur Weigold of the Torrington Creamery donated ice cream served at dinner on Sundays. The camp week culminated on Saturday afternoons, when the boys participated in a Water Meet, while many visitors and parents looked on. The Scouts competed in the breast stroke, back stroke, and diving. For the final event in the Water Meet, the staff hid a watermelon along the shore of West Hill Pond, and the boys sought it out. The winning Scout shared the melon with his tent mates at the evening hot dog roast, which wrapped up the week's program.

STAFF IN FRONT OF THE CAMP'S FLAGPOLE, DURING THE EARLY 1930S, LIKELY IN 1931: Standing fourth from the left in the top row is Chef Carter Bell; many early campers noted his cooking as the high point of Workcoeman. In the bottom row, Seymour Weeks is kneeling second from the left, Edward Jacot third from the left, and V. M. Koonz may be fifth from the left.

Visitors and Baseball

On the tenth of July 1932, Camp Workcoeman opened during the darkest point of the Great Depression. The preceding months saw unemployment reach never before seen highs and industrial production drop to new lows. Throughout March 1932, the Scouts of the Northern Litchfield County Council canvassed Torrington to find work for the unemployed. As people moved to find work, or struggled to keep their businesses open, the council lost volunteers. In the fall of 1931, John Calder, who coordinated much of the Council's expansion, died of heart disease. Calder had ignored his symptoms and instead focused of the difficulties of the Torrington Company.

The deflation made it tough for the Northern Litchfield County Council to gather together the funds for summer camp. As such, the council chose to operate Camp Workcoeman for a shorter four-week season. Over the course of the summer, many visitors to camp helped to ease the financial burden by donating supplies, especially food. These visitors were so numerous that the campers built a picnic area for them. More than eight hundred and fifty people visited camp during the 1932 season. In addition to parents and friends of Scouting, the Scout Mothers' Auxiliary and the Torrington Rotary sent large delegations to Workcoeman. There were also many informal visits, especially from the summer residents around West Hill Pond. While some only stopped by to fill up at Workcoeman's pump, others

Scouts on Workcoeman's parade ground, during the spring of 1932

visited for the Thursday campfire; some even paddled across the lake and watched the program from their canoes.

Baseball, central to the camp program since 1924, was larger than ever during the summer of 1932. Even as boys circulated in and out of camp as one week moved to the next, two teams continued to play each other over the course of the summer, the Hot Cha's and the Steam Rollers. At the end of July, the ballplayers rowed Workcoeman's fleet of seven boats down the lake to face the Hartford Council's Camp Pioneer. Workcoeman led in the first few innings, but Pioneer gained the upper hand when the game was called, in the midst of a heavy mid-summer cloudburst.

Three Cheers for Old Workcoeman

As the Great Depression dragged on through the months of 1933, the Northern Litchfield County Council continued to grow. With work hard to find for most men, boys no longer were able to hold part-time positions, or find summer jobs as farm hands. While this left more time for Scouting, it also made it more difficult to pay for a week of summer camp. Since the council was also strapped for cash, it only opened Workcoeman for four weeks in 1933. In view of the fact that the number of Scouts in the council had increased by fifty percent over 1929, each week ran at full capacity. While the council advertised the record weekly attendances, the reality was that the Dining Hall was crowded.

As people adjusted to job sharing under the National Recovery Administration, citizens who held onto jobs found more time on their hands, some of which they spent as Scouters. The Northern Litchfield County Council received accolades for having the highest level of volunteer participation in New England. A possible side product of this increased volunteer time was a camp song, composed by Amy MacNeil. MacNeil was the mother of a Troop 23 Scout and the wife of the Troop's Assistant Scoutmaster, both Harry MacNeil. The song, *Camp Workcoeman*, is sung to the tune of *The Battle*

Hymn of the Republic. The words describe Workcoeman as a good old camp, already in its tenth season. MacNeil also chose to honor the camp's standards, which may refer to flags, but more likely recall the high bar set for Workcoeman's program.

From the hillside and the valley, from the farm and city too;
Come our boys to old Workcoeman, Scouts that are so fine and true;
And they welcome each new buddy with a handclasp and a smile;
At good old Workcoeman.

Give three cheers for old Workcoeman.
Give three cheers for old Workcoeman.
Give three cheers for old Workcoeman.
Its fame goes marching on.

As years shall come and years shall go, may Scouts that gather here;
Keep the standards of Workcoeman, that are known both far and near;
May they be both true and loyal, grateful to its founders too;
Its name goes marching on.

Scouts on the camp dock during the 1930s, practicing the prone-pressure technique of artificial respiration

Dining Hall Expansion Plans

During the record-breaking winter of 1933–1934, when temperatures in Northwest Connecticut went more than twenty-below zero, the Northern Litchfield County Council conducted its annual financial drive. Even though the economy was as hot as the outside temperature, the council was able to gather enough funds to open Camp Workcoeman for five weeks. This was one more week than in the recent depression years, but still one less week than the prosperous 1920s. The council camping committee hoped that the extra week would relieve some of the crowding, but when the season opened, Workcoeman was at capacity. Years before, the size of the dining hall set the capacity at forty-four, but during the third week of camp, sixty-two scouts attended.

Since the bumper season of 1928, the camping committee argued for an expanded dining hall at each budget cycle, and was turned down. Most members of the council were wary, especially because the dining hall was only a few years old. However, the camping committee found support from the Scout Mothers' Auxiliary as early as 1930. The Auxiliary offered what we would now call a leadership gift, when its president Jennie Coe declared, "We are now ready to provide the fireplace as soon as the council is ready to provide the building to go around it."

With the knowledge of some money on hand and several consecu-

SCOUTS FROM TROOP 2 PLAYING BASEBALL ON THE PARADE GROUND IN THE MIDDLE 1930S

tive high attendance seasons, the council could commit to a dramatic expansion of Camp Workcoeman. Even if the economy continued its slow march to recovery, it would not be easy to raise the funds. The council would have to keep its regular expenses down and save the surplus for several years. While Jennie Coe was a driving force behind the Scout Mothers' Auxiliary's effort to expand Workcoeman, she did not live to see the new dining hall. During the fourth week of camp, she fell down a flight of stairs at her summer home on Bantam Lake, dying in the accident. Camp Workcoeman's trustees and Council Executive Edward Jacot served as pallbearers at the funeral. As Jennie Coe was lowered into the grave, beside her husband Frank, an honor guard of Scouts gave her a final salute.

The Silver Jubilee

"The year 1935 marks the twenty-fifth birthday celebration of the Boy Scouts of America. During these years the value of our organization in building character and in training for citizenship has made itself a vital factor in the life of America" noted Franklin Roosevelt on the eighth of February, when he spoke over a country-wide radio broadcast to commemorate the Silver Jubilee. President Roosevelt then went on to invite 30,000 Scouts from across the land to the District of Columbia for a National Jamboree. Chief Scout Executive James West then asked the boys listening in to unite in pledging the Scout oath. In the Torrington High School Auditorium, four hundred of the six hundred Scouts of the Northern Litchfield County Council joined in with boys across the nation. The excitement of 1935 carried over to local affairs as well; just before the camp season opened, the council Scouts again united to march in the Connecticut Tercentenary parade through the streets of Torrington.

With the uncertain possibility of economic recovery, and the council trying to raise funds for a new dining hall, Camp Workcoeman operated under an unusual schedule in 1935. As in 1934, the council budget allowed for a five-week season, but only three weeks of the traditional program was offered. During the fourth week, camp was open to all, but with an eye towards boys who could not afford the seven-dollar weekly fee. Scouts could attend on a daily basis, for seventy-five cents at a time. Instead of a fifth week, the staff put together a four-day program for the Jamboree Contingent. While the boys got a chance to participate in the usual hiking and swimming, the twenty-five Scouts spent most of their time practicing for their songs for the Region One opening show.

    Scouts who applied to attend the Jamboree were required to get vaccines for smallpox and typhoid fever. No such inoculation for Polio existed, and while the Jamboree Contingent was at Workcoeman, an outbreak occurred in North Carolina. Cases spread into Virginia, and then, just ten days before Scouts were to arrive, appeared in the capital area; the Jamboree was canceled. Fortunately, the national council had scraped together enough funds to insure the event, so the boys and the councils were reimbursed for their fees. On the evening the Jamboree was supposed to open, Scouts were offered a nation-wide radio hookup, and listened to a broadcast of some of the songs written for the Jamboree. It did not quite alleviate the disappointment, but the boys still were able to sing along and hear some of the dramatic programs.

A CAMP BROCHURE FROM 1935, MAILED TO THE PARENTS OF SCOUTS THROUGHOUT THE NORTHERN LITCHFIELD COUNTY COUNCIL: The illustration is based on Henry and John Hintermeister's painting for the cover of the 1929 *Handbook For Patrol Leaders*.

Council Executives

Hardly any Scouters in the Northern Litchfield County Council noticed when Arthur Marston, executive of the Waterbury Council, died of a heart attack on Memorial day, 1935. Most volunteers in Northwest Connecticut were caught up in their own celebrations, and the fervor surrounding the Silver Jubilee. To those who did take note, it seemed like yet another of unfortunate events down the Naugatuck Valley. The Waterbury Council's Camp, Sepunkum, was on government property in Mt. Tom State Park. As the park expanded under Governor Wilbur Cross' unique take on the New Deal, the council had to seek new camping facilities.

With the Waterbury Council Executive's death, the Region One Office in Boston started calling the shots. Before they approved a new executive, the regional office pressured the Waterbury Council to merge with the neighboring Naugatuck Council, which might also take care of the Naugatuck Council's issues. As the new executive, the Regional Office proposed David Babson, exccutive of the Holyoke Council in Massachusetts. None of this seemed particularly important to the volunteers in the Northern Litchfield County Council. Perhaps they found it typical of a regional office that pressured them to dramatically expand in 1929, under the threat of dissolution. Overall, this was part of a larger trend in the BSA, of greater national involvement in local affairs. The National Council had spent most of the past fifteen years attempting to form local councils, to serve every troop in the county. Caught up in that campaign, they left most of the established councils alone. With that program accomplished, there was a growing concern about the independence some councils were asserting. In Region One, this was especially the apparent in the Narragansett Council, with its long tenured executive, J. Harold Williams. Williams offered his own take on the camping program and occasionlly mocked James West at professional development conferences. To replace David Babson in Holyoke, the Regional Office proposed the Northern Litchfield County Council's own executive, Edward Jacot. Jacot had served as Council Executive for eight years, and as Scoutmaster of Troop 1 prior to that. He was one of three long-term Council Executives the Holyoke Council could choose from; they all offered experience, but their transfer would also ensure a degree of independence from the volunteers.

Jacot was only the most recent Scouter turned professional in the Northern Litchfield County Council. All of his predecessors, except Earle Beebe, started as volunteers in Torrington troops. Some of the Executive Board and many members of the council wanted to hire another local man, but were put off by the Region One Office. Instead of selecting from an approved list, the Executive Board was offered one candidate, Palmer Liddle. Liddle was not without qualifications; an Eagle Scout, he worked for two councils in New York, before serving as executive of Maine's Katahdin Council. The board met Liddle on Armistice Day and after some debate about the lack of choice, hired him. Liddle was introduced to the Scouts at a Farewell Party for Jacot, with four hundred in attendance. Before departing for Massachusetts, Jacot thanked the volunteers for their service and said, "I assure you, we shall never forget you and will always look upon Litchfield county as our old home."

Scouts assembled for tent inspection during the mid 1930s: Council Executive Palmer Liddle at right.

Palmer Liddle

Camp Workcoeman opened on 5 July 1936 with a new camp director, Council Executive Palmer Liddle. The new executive had taught canoeing at Spruce Ridge Scout Camp, and worked within program and in administration at Camp Roosevelt and Camp Syracuse. Liddle was not hired for his camp experience, but more likely for his successes in growing rural troops. The previous executive, Edward Jacot, had built up a strong organization in Torrington, and to a lesser extent in Winsted, but the troops in the farm communities were relatively small. On the other hand, Liddle had a good deal of success in bucolic organization in the Onondaga Council and the Orange-Sullivan Council.

At Workcoeman in 1936, Liddle expanded the camp program to a full week, with Scouts entering and leaving camp on Sunday afternoons. However, Liddle maintained most of the traditional activities, such as the Thursday evening campfires. In practice, Clarence Rosenbeck, Aquatics Director since 1932, was in charge of the program. Rosenbeck emphasized sports and aquatics, and the boys competed against the best of Camp Sequessen on Thursdays. The extended schedule allowed for the return of a hiking program, and during the lightly attended week one, the campers and staff went on a fourteen-mile hike.

Meanwhile, Palmer Liddle focused on administration and facil-

TROOP 2 SCOUTS AT CAMP DURING THE MID 1930S

ities. The Northern Litchfield County Council had been talking about expanding the dining hall for more than six years. Over those years, the council set aside small sums of money, but not nearly enough for a substantial construction. The 1936 council fund drive had come up short, which after several years of depression seemed normal. However, 1936 was the first year that Gross Domestic Product was on par with 1929 levels. A new executive and economic recovery might bring the rapping of hammers back to the woods near West Hill Pond.

A New Dining Hall

1937 was a year for second chances. The National Council resolved to go back to the District of Columbia and host another jamboree. In Connecticut, the local Scouters had been discussing building a new dining hall at Camp Workcoeman since the bumper season of 1928. National canceled the 1935 Jamboree because of a polio outbreak, but the Northern Litchfield County Council just didn't have any money. During anniversary week in February of 1937, the National Council committed to a three hundred and fifty-acre encampment, and just two weeks prior, the Northern Litchfield County Council declared that the campers of 1937 would greet a brand new building at Workcoeman.

    The years of economic depression kept the Northern Litchfield County Council from expanding either its programs or facilities. After a few years of saving, the building fund only contained three hundred and fifty dollars. Years had passed since the annual financial campaign met its goal. However, there was a sense of possibility; towards the end of the previous year Gross Domestic Product neared 1929 levels. Unemployment was at its lowest levels in years, even if there were twice as many unemployed as when people first started talking about a new dining hall. In 1937, the council started it annual campaign three months sooner than the previous year, and raised the goal from $5,000 to $6,000. Council Executive Palmer Liddle called in Hillard Holbrook, Deputy Regional Scout Executive, to help plan the campaign. They set up on a passionate ten-day drive in Torrington, with sixteen teams of four to six volunteers circulating throughout the city. Smaller, but just as intense drives in the outlying communities over the following months would complete the campaign. To justify the twenty percent increase, the Scouters made Camp Workcoeman central to their plea. They connected improved facilities to the greater Scouting program, and without these amenities, boys would only be able to use Workcoeman in the summer. As with the previous years, the campaign did not meet its goal, but only just. The Council raised more money than even in the prosperous years of the 1920s.

The Torrington campaign brought in enough money to meet all of the regular budget items; thus, all of the funds raised in the small town campaigns could go directly to the new dining hall. Yet, the successful drive brought in only six-hundred and fifty dollars to start the build. That did not go very far towards the $4,500 structure that Architect Carl Johnson was designing. To save money, the twenty-eight by forty-eight foot structure would abut the old dining hall, which would be transformed into a kitchen. Taking advantage of the geology, the plans called for a foundation of fieldstone piers. Even with the financial constraints, the structure was not completely utilitarian; an open veranda would run the entire length of the east side of the building and overlook the lake. Connecticut Light and Power would run electrical lines along the old wood road and up to the old dining hall, with the help of the summer residents. However, the highlight of the structure would be a massive fieldstone fireplace in the east wall, the same five hundred dollar fireplace that Jennie Coe and the Scout Mothers' Auxiliary had raised the funds for back in 1930.

Construction started at the end of June, just as the Jamboree

Troop was conducting its shakedown at Workcoeman. Not far from the excavation site, the Scouts and Scouters practiced their own construction, a bridge for their campsite gateway on Columbia Island. On the second to last day of the Jamboree, the Northern Litchfield County council was $2,500 short of the total cost. The economic recovery that seemed apparent when the Scouters started the drive was now uncertain. It turned out that the unemployment low in November of 1936 was not a trend towards growth, but an acme, before the economy slipped back into recession. Even without all the funds on hand, the Torrington Building Company finished the structure as planned, and in time for the opening of camp on the nineteenth of July. Even by the time the building was dedicated on Tuesday of week three, it was not yet paid for. Still, that did not seem to matter too much. The hall was quite impressive, with its substantial fireplace, polished maple floor, and most of all, its capacity. During weeks two and three of 1937, about sixty Scouts attended; however, the new dining hall could hold more than double that number. The Scouters of the Northern Litchfield County Council were thinking long term; they would pay the costs in a few years, depression or prosperity. They were confident in Workcoeman's future, and hopeful for future of Scouting in Connecticut.

THE SOUTH SIDE OF THE NEW DINING HALL, IN THE FALL OF 1937 OR THE SPRING OF 1938

1938 Season

Camp Workcoeman's new dining hall proved to be a valuable addition during the summer of 1938, hosting many a campfire. More than half of the camp season was rainy, and the downpours were so fierce that the camp road washed away. There was so much precipitation towards the end of the second week, and more predicted for week three, that many Scouts moved their reservations to week four. To compensate, the Northern Litchfield County Council offered a special week three discount, in which Scouts could attend for the rest of the third week at a dollar a day. In spite of the rain, overall camp attendance was up. The Scouts let it rain and carried on in the dining hall, filling the big room with the spirit of fifty boys.

The new, larger dining hall could seat around one hundred and twenty people, and the size of the building reflected the farsightedness of the council volunteers. The Scouters of the Northern Litchfield County Council expected that camp attendance would slowly grow to fill the hall. To prepare for a larger future, in 1938 the Camping Committee divided the tenting area into three individual campsites, which they called villages. Perhaps coming close to what Frank Coe meant by a permanent camp, the council built three Adirondack Shelters in one site, with the intention of replacing all of the tents with shelters as the canvas wore out. These new shelters served as an incentive; the shelters were only open to Scouts who registered early. As another enticement, a Scout who signed up for the sparsely attended week one could arrive at camp two days early, a nine day program at a seven day price. As a final incentive, the Camping Committee offered a one-dollar discount for early registrations. When a full camp of fifty boys arrived on the eighth of July, they named the Adirondack village Rocky Ledge. The Scouts picked Poplar Grove and Camp Wasuwanee for the other two sites. The three camp villages allowed the staff to play up the competitive angle, not only in sports, such as soccer, volleyball, and softball, but also in Scouting skills. The staff also offered several season long contests for individual Scouts; the horseshoe championship was probably the most contested, but the fire by friction competition was an especially difficult contest. Clarence Rosenbeck did not return for the 1938 season, as he entered full-time employment. Therefore, the Camping Committee and Council Executive Palmer Liddle recruited Carl Bergquist as Assistant Camp Director and W. Whitney Tileston as the first formal Program Director. In addition to his summer camp experience, Bergquist directed the physical education programs for the public schools in Webster, Massachusetts. Tileston served as Music Director for Litchfield High School and the town's grammar schools. Camp veteran Raymond French was promoted to Aquatics Director, after ten days of training at Camp Brooklyn. Like his predecessors, French emphasized swimming instruction, and the overall camp program was similar to past years. Perhaps thanks to Tileston, there was a greater emphasis on the campfire programs, especially the closing campfire on Saturday evenings. However, with many visitors in attendance at the Thursday campfire, Scouts tended to think of the earlier one as the major campfire. Wednesday evenings saw one new addition to the camp program, a film screening. Scouts watched a variety of movies ranging from *The Complete Life of the Bee and the Making of Honey*, to films from John Houlihan's vacation in

ROCKY LEDGE CAMPSITE IN THE LATE 1930S: Rocky Ledge occupied the present site of the Scoutmasters' Cabin, while Poplar Grove was immediately to the north-east of the current Nature Lodge.

South America. However, on the last Wednesday of the summer, Flieg and Newbury, Incorporated, offered the boys a special treat, a Laurel and Hardy short, along with cartoons of Popeye and Mickey Mouse.

Building Boom

During the late 1930s, Camp Workcoeman underwent a building boom. In 1937, the Northern Litchfield County Council built a $4,500 dining hall and the next year added a campsite with three Adirondack shelters. However, that growth was limited to structures, not attendance. The average number of Scouts in camp in the 1930s was no greater than during the late 1920s, but the Boy Scout membership in Litchfield County increased by seventy percent in the ten years since 1929. In those ten years, two recessions and anemic growth weighed down the economy, making it difficult to come up with the seven dollar camp fee. In 1939, industrial production again reached 1929 levels, and recovery finally seemed a real possibility. That uncertain prosperity helped the Northern Litchfield County Council to raise enough funds to pay off the last of its debt from the dining hall construction. However, the council would have to act if that growth was to bring about an increase in camp turnout.

As a way of promoting the ninth point of the Scout law and increasing attendance, the council offered a camp savings plan in 1939. Modeled on the United States Postal Savings System, each Scout was issued a booklet with spaces for 70 stamps. For each dime he deposited with the council office, the Scout was one stamp closer to filling his booklet. The council hoped that if a boy could see his progress towards a week of camp, he would be more likely to attend, and more likely to develop a lifelong habit of thrift.

The boys who entered Workcoeman in 1939 dropped their gear into new Adirondack shelters before heading to the waterfront for a swim test. That year, the Council built four shelters in the Poplar Grove Village, adding to the three shelters constructed in Rocky Ledge Village the year before. That summer, the only canvas in camp was for the handicraft tent. In addition to retiring the World War One surplus tents, the Camping Committee also retired Camp Wasuwanee Village, which had only gained its name the previous year, but had housed campers for many seasons. Two campsites made it quite a bit easier for the staff to organize camp sports. While volleyball was the more popular in 1939, the new rivalry extended to the traditional camp sport—baseball. Of course, when challenged by another camp, the Scouts could play together; at the end of week three, the Workcoeman boys headed off to the Alfred W. Dater Council's Camp Toquam, on Dog Pond in Goshen, to challenge the home team. The Scouts managed to finish the game before a thundershower, but the home team stormed ahead and won the intercamp contest.

Scouts at the waterfront in the late 1930s

Growing Nationalism

Just a few weeks after the end of the 1939 camp season, Germany and the Soviet Union invaded Poland. The following spring, Germany invaded Denmark, Norway, and France, and the Soviet Union invaded Finland. Those events shook the American people's non-interventionist tendencies, and an improbable presidential hopeful, Wendell Willkie, campaigned on supporting Britain right up to the cusp of war. Both those opposing intervention and those for it called upon an American nationalism to justify themselves. The non-interventionists recalled George Washington's warning about entangling alliances, and the interventionist tried to rally their countrymen to support democracy around the world.

In the Northern Litchfield County Council, the Air Forces of the Second World War inspired events such as model airplane meets. The growing patriotic feeling manifested itself in American History pageants and in the Workcoeman campfire programs. Whereas in the 1930s campfires included instrumental selections and songs like "John Jacob Jingleheimer Schmidt," in 1940 campfires opened with "My Country, 'Tis of Thee" and closed with "God Bless America."

The 1940 summer program offered an increased number of activities for more experienced Scouts. These veteran Scouts were assigned to the Rocky Ledge campsite, while the tenderfeet stayed in Poplar Grove. The smaller group in the Rocky Ledge Campsite was easier to

SCOUTS ASSEMBLED ON THE PARADE GROUND DURING THE 1930S

accommodate on outpost treks. These Scouts left for a hike each Tuesday Morning, returning the following day. This new emphasis on older Scouts allowed some of the more experienced canoers to head to Winchester and paddle around Highland Lake. These programs may have factored into increased attendance in 1940; that summer, weeks two and three were filled to capacity, and during week four there were more Scouts in camp than bunks in Adirondack Shelters.

Economic Recovery

After twelve years of depression, the American economy finally recovered by 1941. Even if the gross domestic product of 1937 exceeded that of 1929, the population increase during those years meant that the average consumer received little comfort from that parity. However, by 1941 gross domestic product per capita exceeded 1929 by ten percent, enough to compensate for the increased government expenditures of New Deal programs and rearmament. That year, the Northern Litchfield County Council set its annual campaign goal at $7,100, and raised enough funds to open Camp Workcoeman for five weeks, the first five week season since 1934.

The stronger economy and the successful fund drive also allowed for facility improvements at camp. The council paid to upgrade the plumbing in the kitchen and replaced the stovetop boiler with running hot water, for washing dishes. Council Finance chairman Floyd Pearce persuaded The Exchange Club of Torrington to donate a Handicraft Lodge to the Scouts; Pearce phrased his pitch as a challenge from the Canaan Exchange Club, who had already committed to buying new rowboats and canoes for Workcoeman. Exchangites donated lumber and helped with most of the construction; one of their number, Herbert Jones, brought his carpentry class from the trade school to camp to complete the rough framing. Club members also installed the hot water system the council bought. The

Exchangites collected used hand tools from Torrington citizens, then repaired and sharpened the tools to supply not only a building but also the materials for a camp program.

To staff the new lodge, Council Executive Palmer Liddle sent Assistant Camp Director Carl Bergquist to National Camping School, to participate in the Handicraft Section. Liddle did not join the 1941 staff himself, and brought in former Aquatics Director Clarence Rosenbeck to serve as Camp Director. Rosenbeck was Scoutmaster of Troop 14 and of the 1937 Jamboree Troop. Back in 1929, Rosenbeck had played camp director when the campers took over Workcoeman's operation. In 1942, he brought back this program feature, and campers ran the Workcoeman program on the third of July. However, the highlight of the first week was a fireworks show, put together by the District One Committee, composed of Scouters from Torrington and Harwinton. The fireworks show helped to boost the numbers of campers during the sparsely attended week one. During the other four weeks, Workcoeman was full, with seventy-five campers, and a season total of one hundred and seventy-four separate Scouts.

HANDICRAFT LODGE DURING THE 1940S: The structure now serves as the Trading Post.

War

The unforeseen strike of the Imperial Japanese Navy on the Pacific Fleet at Pearl Harbor transformed the United States from an arsenal of democracy to a full-fledged combatant. In Torrington, boys were trained as messengers, in case of communication failures during air raids. Most of the participants were Scouts, but since the Chief Air Raid Warden sought six-hundred boys over the age of fourteen, and the total membership of the Northern Litchfield County Council was only seven hundred and fifty, youth from other Boys' Clubs partook as well. In one session of the training, the boys witnessed a demonstration of incendiary bombs, and saw how fires that could not be doused with water could be extinguished. This fear of an air attack on Torrington's war industries kept the city on edge; although Northwest Connecticut was far outside of the blackout zone, the area three miles from the New England coast where the government required citizens to dim all lights visible from the ocean, the city underwent several practice blackouts during 1942.

 The fear of air raids decreased with the distance from Pearl Harbor, and Scouts focused more on resource collection than on civil defense. To supply the United States its own airplanes, the boys of the Northern Litchfield County Council, in cooperation with the Torrington-Litchfield Girl Scout Council, went door-to-door collecting aluminum. In addition to metals, the Scouts collected rags and rubber for recycling. In June of 1942, Council Executive Palmer Liddle was commissioned as a Lieutenant in the Air Division of the United States Navy. Liddle may have been pursuing a commission for some time, perhaps as early as 1941, when he recruited Clarence Rosenbeck to direct Camp Workcoeman. Before the Council Executive resigned, he hired Carl Bergquist, Assistant Director for four years, to take the helm for the summer.

For most members of the Boy Scouts of America, the main concern during the summer of 1942 was getting to camp. Scouts of the 1920s often took trolleys part of the way to their camp, but most of these lines went bankrupt during the Great Depression. In the 1940s, an automobile ride was the predominate way to go camping, but wartime restrictions complicated that journey. Gasoline rationing made the hundred mile round trip to the New Britain Area Council's Camp Keemosahbee difficult. Even more of a challenge was the one hundred and fifty mile circuit for the boys of Stamford's Alfred W. Dater Council. However, unlike most Scout councils, the Northern Litchfield County Council's Camp Workcoeman was within its jurisdiction. For the population centers of Winsted and Torrington, Workcoeman was five and seven miles away, respectively. Scouts could easily carpool, and the Scout Mothers' Auxiliary revived its original mission, providing transportation to Boy Scout activities. Without gasoline, camp was a half-day hike, even for a dilatory tenderfoot. While most Scout camps had to cut back their programs during the Second World War, Workcoeman's location allowed it to maintain attendance, and even expand.

> # BOY SCOUTS
> ## Your Help Is Needed!
> The Torrington Salvage Committee Needs Your Assistance Saturday Morning At 8:30 O'clock.
>
> Report At City Hall to Assist in Collecting Scrap for Defense.

ENCOURAGING PARTICIPATION IN WAR SERVICE: From page nine of the *Torrington Register* of 29 July 1942.

New Leadership

With the intensifying of the Second World War, Council Executive Palmer Liddle entered the United States Navy in 1942. The Northern Litchfield County Council searched for a new chief and hired a Mainer, E. Merle Hildreth. Much like Liddle, Hildreth was recruited from the Katahdin Council, where he previously worked as Assistant Scout Executive and Field Executive. In the first days of 1943, the council doubled its professional staff by hiring Nathaniel Doten. Doten, formerly a Field Executive in Massachusetts' Sachem Council, was to focus on Scouting in Winsted and build up Northwest Connecticut's Cubbing program.

Chief Hildreth and Nat Doten not only brought new faces to Camp Workcoeman, but also a new twist to the camp program. For most of previous seasons, a boy's time at camp emphasized athletics and aquatics, with scoutcraft training left mostly to his troop. In 1943, Workcoeman offered a great deal more basic skill instruction, with a special focus on cooking. That summer, every Scout had to prepare at least one meal for himself. This tied into a larger theme of preparedness, not just because of the Second World War, but also to encourage each boy to be self-sufficient.

The new professional staff also developed a unique theme for each of the five weeklong sessions. These different themes catered to the many Scouts who spent two weeks, three weeks, or even the

1943 CAMP PATCH: First of the seasonally issued emblems.

whole summer at Workcoeman. The first week, commando week, fit in well with the preparedness emphasis. Boys learned wilderness first aid, marksmanship, tracking, and map making and trained in an obstacle course. Some of the others weekly themes included King Neptune's Court and the Olympic Games. However, the highlight of the summer was Magic Carpet Week, wherein the Scouts were transported to exotic locals, experiencing festivities from around the world and across time. The boys of 1943 experienced the world from Mexico to India, from Sherwood Forest to Brazilian Carnival. At the end of the summer, Chief Hildreth instituted a new camp honor society at the final campfire. As part of an investiture ceremony, the boys acted out the Iroquois creation legend. The ceremony and the summer closed as the Scouts danced to the beat of a water-drum.

Helping the War Effort

As the Second World War raged in Africa, Europe, and the Pacific, more and more Connecticutians entered the Armed Forces. In the farms throughout the Northern Litchfield County Council's territory, the lack of farm workers left much of the crops in the fields. While just a few years prior, the depression prevented most Scouts from finding a job, but the Department of Agriculture offered summer jobs especially for Scouts, even offering to truck them to Maine to help with the potato harvest. While some boys worked during the summer, the largest need was in the fall when the apples ripened. Seventy Scouts of the Northern Litchfield County Council volunteered to hike out to Bantam and pick the apples, and were let out of school to complete the task.

For the summer of 1944, the Council cooperated with the Mattatuck Council of Waterbury to operate a farm camp. The camp combined farm work with a Scouting program and was promoted as a leadership development program for boys over the age of fourteen. The Scouts got a chance to stay at Columbia University's camp near Bantam Lake. The farm camp opened as soon as school dismissed in June and operated up until Workcoeman opened.

The labor shortage struck the Council in December of 1943 when Assistant Executive Nathaniel Doten was drafted into the Army. Over the next few months, the council tried to recruit another profes-

DINING HALL FIREPLACE DURING THE SUMMER OF 1944

sional, but the position remained unfilled until September. Workcoeman's summer program was affected as well; the only adults on the Summer Staff were Chief Merle Hildreth and Scoutmaster Seymour Weeks. However, this gave many of the boys who worked at the farm camp a chance to try out their leadership skills as staff at Workcoeman. The toughest position to fill was camp chef, as so many of the people who could prepare meals in quantity were cooking for the Armed Forces. Even a renovated kitchen and a new Cook's Cabin could not attract a chef; therefore, Chief Hildreth's wife, Mary, prepared the meals that summer.

Expansion

When the Northern Litchfield County Council's executive, Merle Hildreth, was hired in 1942, among his first tasks was to develop a plan to grow the council. In addition to increasing enrollment and developing the nascent Cubbing program, this five-year plan also included improvements at Camp Workcoeman. Chief Hildreth worked with the newly elected Council President Edward Diddler and Finance Chairman Floyd Pearce to raise $10,000 to upgrade camp. The National Council's Engineering Division and its Health and Safety Service visited Camp and proposed new constructions. The Council also worked with local foresters to create a land management plan, and for each of the five years, Scouts planted 1,000 trees at camp. The money slowly trickled in and a new waterfront, a Cook's Cabin, and the Tunxis Campsite were built, but the largest expansion was the following year.

As the United Nations edged closer to victory during 1945, the prospects for a brighter future caught on in Northwest Connecticut. That year, the Northern Litchfield County Council recruited enough boys to complete its five-year plan—in three years. The funds that the council raised that year also allowed it to complete a new parking area to the South of the Parade Ground, a Chief's Cabin near the water's edge, a Pioneer Campsite, and a Scoutmasters' Cabin in the former Rocky Ledge Campsite. These were not simply housing, but included program components as well. For example, the Scoutmasters' Cabin was not a place for the Scoutmasters to sleep, but an incentive to attend camp with their troop. Troop 15 of Cornwall attended camp as a troop in the late 1930s, and the Scouts in Troop 2 of Torrington and Troop 34 of Winsted usually went in their regular patrols, but since 1924, most Scouts attended as individuals. Chief Hildreth wanted the summer program to better compliment the troop's year-round program; a troop that attended camp in a body, with all of its patrols, could develop into a better, more organized unit. As an inducement, a Scoutmaster who came to camp with his whole troop could bring along his wife and other family members; these non-Scouts could take their meals in the Dining Hall and stay in the Scoutmasters' Cabin for a vacation along West Hill Pond.

Even with the many new constructions at camp and the new unit emphasis, much of the camp program followed the lines of the twenty years prior. The new program of 1943 did not catch on, and the themed weeks were set aside. The emphasis on scoutcraft basics and a few of the special events, however, remained. For instance, during the first week of camp in 1945, the campwide game was "the conquest of Mars." For Monday afternoon, half the Scouts were Martians and successfully repelled an attack by the other half of camp—Earthmen who tried to land their stratoplane on the surface of Mars. Overall, the traditional stress on aquatics and athletics returned for the 1945 season, even if a number of Scouts attended in a new context, with their troop. The mid 1940s camp expansion prepared Workcoeman for the post-war period, such as the new parking lot, which accommodated the suburbanization of the 1950s. In addition, many of the donations for the campaign came in the form of war bonds, which could supply funds for Camp Workcoeman into the coming decade.

CHIEF HILDRETH DURING THE CONSTRUCTION OF THE PARKING AREA, IN FRONT OF WHAT IS NOW THE TRADING POST

Post-War Prosperity

The restrictions of the Second World War constrained most American Scout camps; however, Workcoeman's distinctions allowed it to prosper. The location near the center of the Northern Litchfield County Council's territory overcame gasoline rationing. This, along with a series of well-orchestrated membership drives, combined to bring camp attendance to record levels. Over three years, the Council Executive Board raised ten thousand dollars to improve the facilities at camp. These factors prepared Workcoeman for heightened activity of the post war years.

In 1946, a group of music teachers from Winsted, East Hartford, and Manchester brought Laurel Music Camp to Workcoeman. The previous summer, Elizabeth Sonier of the Gilbert School in Winsted organized a choir program on Highland lake. For 1946, she and Wallace Wagner recruited music teachers from around the state, who in turn brought their students to West Hill Pond. A total of forty-eight students attended, and performed under guest conductor Marlowe Smith of Rochester.

This one-week of music camp was not the only group to use Workcoeman; since the 1930s, the local Girl Scout Council operated a week-long day camp after the Boy Scout season ended. However, when Bernie Moore was hired as the new Girl Scout professional, she developed a full camping program at Workcoeman. Down the

SCOUTS AT THE WATERFRONT DURING THE LATE 1940S

Naugatuck Valley, the Housatonic Council shut down its summer program at Camp Irvine and struck a deal to send their boys to Workcoeman. These varied programs made the late 1940s some of the most active summers at Workcoeman. With the five weeks of Boy Scout resident camp, two weeks of Girl Scout camp, Laurel Music Camp, and a week of training, some of the staff spent nine weeks at Workcoeman.

Made in the USA
Charleston, SC
07 July 2014